Teens
and
SOCIAL MEDIA

By Bonnie Hinman

ReferencePoint
Press®

San Diego, CA

TEEN
Health
and
Safety

© 2019 ReferencePoint Press, Inc.
Printed in the United States

For more information, contact:
ReferencePoint Press, Inc.
PO Box 27779
San Diego, CA 92198
www.ReferencePointPress.com

Content Consultant: Scottye J. Cash, MSSW, Ph.D., Associate Professor of Social Work, The Ohio State University

LIBRARY OF CONGRESS CATALOGING-IN-PUBLICATION DATA

Name: Hinman, Bonnie, author.
Title: Teens and Social Media / by Bonnie Hinman.
Description: San Diego, CA : ReferencePoint Press, [2019] | Series: Teen
  Health and Wellness | Includes bibliographical references and index.
Identifiers: LCCN 2018011552 (print) | LCCN 2018020116 (ebook) | ISBN
  9781682825129 (ebook) | ISBN 9781682825112 (hardback)
Subjects: LCSH: Internet and teenagers—Juvenile literature.
Classification: LCC HQ799.2.I5 (ebook) | LCC HQ799.2.I5 H56 2019 (print) |
  DDC 004.67/80835—dc23
LC record available at https://lccn.loc.gov/2018011552

CONTENTS

Introduction

THE NEW
VIRTUAL WORLD

In June 2017, Harvard University announced that it had canceled admission offers to at least ten incoming freshmen. The reason: the students had shared offensive images within what they thought was a private Facebook group chat. The images that the students posted made fun of child abuse, the Holocaust, minority groups, and sexual assault. Harvard evidently did not believe that students who would exhibit this kind of behavior would make good Harvard material. That sounds reasonable to most adults, but the students involved were probably shocked. They were high achievers with good grades. Without those attributes, an Ivy League school like Harvard would not have accepted them.

The teens claimed to be joking around. Their conversation was supposed to be a private Facebook chat. They were sending memes to one another. Memes are images or videos with captions. They are often funny or sarcastic. The teens were trying to be funny by posting offensive memes. Each teenager tried to outdo the others. If questioned, they might say that they didn't share the beliefs in their memes. However, the students had ignored one important rule of social media: nothing online is ever private. Their misconception of privacy cost them dearly. Their poor judgment doomed their entrance into Harvard University.

Researchers say that some areas of teenagers' brains develop more slowly than other areas do. Journalist and minister Judith Johnson explains, "With an underdeveloped prefrontal cortex, a teenager's decision making is less likely to successfully weigh outcomes, form judgments, and control impulses and emotions." Johnson goes on to say, "At the same time, they have a fairly well-developed nucleus accumbens (the area of the brain that seeks pleasure and reward)."[1] Teens may look physically mature, but they have a few more years to go before they are adults in every way. The risks of this immaturity are evident in the world of social media.

> **"With an underdeveloped prefrontal cortex, a teenager's decision making is less likely to successfully weigh outcomes, form judgments, and control impulses and emotions."[1]**
>
> —Judith Johnson, journalist and minister

Digital Natives

Today's teenagers are digital natives. They have grown up with computers, smartphones, and tablets. As toddlers they may have watched Thomas the Tank Engine videos on their parents' computers. Perhaps their parents rejoiced at having a few minutes of quiet, free from toddler demands. By the time they were ten or eleven, many of today's teens were lobbying for their own computers, tablets, and smartphones. They may have said they needed the computers and tablets to do research for school. The phones, they may have argued, would be useful for emergency calls. Parents often agreed to provide the devices. All parents want their children to have the tools they need

A teen takes a selfie at home to share with her friends. Sharing photos and videos has become one of the most common uses of social media.

to do well in school and to call for help in an emergency. As the kids entered their teen years, they knew what social media was even if they did not yet use it or know the name for it.

Facebook was one of the first social networking websites to claim millions of worldwide users. In 2004, Facebook founder Mark Zuckerberg designed Facebook to be a virtual photo directory for Harvard University students. The college students used it to keep in touch with one another. They posted photos and much of their private information. They posted things such as dormitory addresses, phone numbers, and class schedules. Initially, the students didn't think it caused any harm to share photos and information that were not appropriate for everyone to see. They believed that since Facebook focused on college students, the only viewers would be other college students.

Facebook's number of users steadily increased. Facebook use spread from Harvard to other college campuses to high schools to everybody else. Facebook and other social networking websites that developed around the same time seemed harmless enough at first. For teens, social media was a fun way to stay in touch with their friends. Some parents didn't mind it, since it seemed to keep their teens in their rooms instead of wandering around malls or other public places, where they might get in trouble.

Doubts about Social Media

It would be years before most parents, teachers, and researchers experienced doubt about social media. Eventually, they saw that more and more teens were becoming anxious and depressed. Statistics showed that the suicide rate for teens was climbing. Parents suspected that their teens' excessive online time was contributing to these problems. Researcher Jean Twenge asked Athena, a thirteen-year-old girl from Houston, Texas, if teens are closer to their parents these days, since the teens spend more time at home on social media. "I've seen my friends with their families—they don't talk to them," Athena said. "They just say 'Okay, okay, whatever' while they're on their phones. They don't pay attention to their family." Athena said she tuned out her parents too. She spent most of her summer vacation socializing with her friends via text or Snapchat. "I've been on my phone more than I've been with actual people," she said. "My bed has, like, an imprint of my body."[2]

Questions abound about social media use. Can a teen become addicted to social media? Does using social media cause depression and anxiety? Perhaps most importantly, can social media drive a teen to suicide? These are some of the questions that parents are asking experts to answer.

Chapter 1

WHAT ARE THE PROBLEMS WITH SOCIAL MEDIA?

Tanner stopped to pick up his friend Josh so they could attend a basketball game. Tanner found his friend crawling around on the floor in the family room, all the while yelling at his younger sister. Josh's phone had disappeared, and by the sound of it, he thought his sister had something to do with it. Josh popped up from behind the couch, red-faced and angry. About that time, Tanner looked up to see Josh's toddler brother trot into the room with the missing phone. Tanner could see that his friend was trying to stay calm, but Josh still grabbed the phone away from his brother.

Look at a middle school or high school common area before school. A few students stand around and talk, but many more are sitting, heads down, looking at their smartphones. Some students play games while others tap wildly on their tiny onscreen keyboards. Schools often require that students leave their phones in their lockers once classes begin. That means there isn't much time to check the latest Instagram posts, stream video on YouTube, or send photos on Snapchat.

These teens are tuning in to the latest fun that the internet can provide. The apps these students use are called social media. Broadly speaking, social media is any user-driven, interactive, web-based form of electronic communication. On social media, users create online communities to share information, ideas, personal messages, and content such as images and videos. While social media includes blogs, message boards, chat rooms, and online games, the term *social media* is most often used to describe electronic social networking services. Facebook, Twitter, Instagram, Snapchat, YouTube, and Pinterest are just a few of many electronic social networking services currently in existence. Social networking is the practice of increasing social contacts by making connections through individual people (often through social media).

Many teens take advantage of free time before and between classes to check into social media. Others use social media during classes, despite school rules against this.

Social media allow users to create and publish content via the internet. Often these services feature user-created personal profiles. Users with similar interests can share information, ideas, messages, and other content. Sharing content is a large part of social media.

The term *social media addiction* has been in widespread use since about 2012. Parents are often the first to use this term to describe how their children spend all their time online, whether on a smartphone, tablet, computer, or other internet-enabled electronic device. Some experts use the term *addiction* as well. They point out that overuse of social media can isolate teens. Isolation can, in turn, lead to depression, anxiety, eating disorders, low self-esteem, and several other physical and mental difficulties.

An addiction is a serious, chronic condition that causes problems in someone's life. More specifically, an addiction is a distinct set of behaviors related to obtaining a substance or doing an activity. This also means that people with addiction experience a distinct set of

POPULAR SOCIAL MEDIA APPS

Snapchat was created to allow users to send photos and videos to each other instantly via their mobile phones. These photos and videos played once to friends for just a few seconds. Then the content disappeared. The app is constantly changing. Users can now replay snaps an unlimited number of times. Users can also screenshot any pictures or videos they want to save. As for the snaps a user sends to someone else, that user can store them in the Memories section of his or her account.

Instagram allows its users to share pictures and videos with their friends. Much of Instagram's popularity comes from its picture editing features. Dozens of Instagram filters allow users to transform images. Users may create profiles that can connect to other platforms, such as Twitter. Users can share photos, videos, hashtag pages, profiles, and locations with one person or several people. Users can post several photos or videos into one story that disappears after twenty-four hours.

Facebook is a more general social networking service than Snapchat or Instagram. Users maintain a friends list and privacy settings to choose who may see their online content. Users may post photos and videos as well as text, and they can stream live videos too. Facebook supports group pages, fan pages, and business pages.

responses when they can no longer get that substance or do that activity. A person with an addiction continues to engage in the same behavior despite persistent consequences.

Researcher Sarah Williams writes that behavioral addictions and substance addictions might be different sides of the same coin: "There is some evidence that behavioral addictions share common biological and behavioral characteristics as substance addictions."[3] However, the American Psychiatric Association (APA) recognizes only gambling disorder as a behavioral addiction. The APA does not recognize other behavioral addictions, such as internet or social media addiction, as official diagnoses for mental disorders.

A person with an addicition cannot get through a day without longing for and searching for a means to get the substance or to engage in the activity that brings him or her so much pleasure. The desire to obtain the substance or activity that causes the pleasure is overwhelming to a person with an addicition.

It's easy to see how parents might conclude that their children are addicted to social media. Their teens' behaviors check off several boxes that are supposed to indicate addiction. More than 70 percent of teens have smartphones. Many teens are on their phones all the time. That includes when they are in bed or while they are in the bathroom. Teens experience negative effects from their excessive use, such as lower grades and less sleep. However, they seldom see the connection of these consequences to social media overuse. So, on the surface, teens' use of social media does sound like addiction.

However, there are many other problems with social media that are not caused by overuse. Even if a teen does not spend too much time on social media, the time he or she does spend there can cause body image problems, lead to bullying, and allow teens to develop an unrealistic picture of other teens' lives.

Disagreement on Addiction

Not everyone agrees that excessive social media use counts as addiction. Scientist danah boyd, who spells her name with all lowercase letters, researches technology and society. She says that the connection between media use and addiction is unclear. "Media coverage of teens' use of social media amplifies the notion that the current generation of youth is uncontrollably hooked on these new technologies and unable to control their lives."[4] boyd goes on to say, "When talking about teens' engagement with social media, many adults use the concept of addiction to suggest that teens lack control."[5] However, boyd isn't so sure that teens lack control—or at least, teens don't lack control as much as adults think. She relates that while some teens do become obsessed with technology, it doesn't mean that using social media always leads to problems for teens.

Media critic Kyle Smith offers a different take on why screen addiction might not be a bad thing. Smith says, "Today it turns out that teens are going out less than ever. Partying less than ever. Getting pregnant less than ever. They are, in fact, spending the years of heedless, extravagant, ebullient youth holed up alone in their bedrooms."[6] Kids are spending more time with parents and forgoing many risky behaviors. Smith wonders if the downsides of smartphones are an acceptable price to pay for such benefits.

Algorithms and Teens

When the internet began, people expected it to be an open source of information. That is, all information would be equally accessible to all users. It hasn't played out that way. In 2004, Google introduced the first personalized content algorithm to its searches. It used browsing history, location, and language to figure out what users meant by the terms they used. In 2011, Facebook started using algorithms to create users' news feeds. These algorithms are designed to show users what they will probably like. Since then, algorithms have more or less taken over the internet. Algorithms are the bits of computer code used to search online posts for matches. That might be a match with a certain product for sale or a match of a political article to a user's expressed political opinions.

Algorithms do make it easier to cope with the huge amount of information on the internet, but they carry some downsides too. A user may end up not seeing what people who think differently see. That user may not even know that a different viewpoint exists. Teens, with their still-developing brains and their relatively small amount of personal experience, can be easily influenced. Seeing only one side of an issue can give them an unrealistic view of the world.

Positive Effects

Some scientists point out social media's positive effects. They say that besides making young people more technologically savvy, social media can boost self-esteem and provide emotional support. It may be particularly helpful for teens who feel that they have no place to belong. Marginalized teens, such as kids in foster homes and LGBTQ adolescents, may make social connections online that they would not be able to find in their everyday lives. Indiana University Media School professor Amy Gonzales says, "We need to think about social media as not being

> **"We need to think about social media as not being absolutely good or bad. We need to think about how to come up with appropriate uses of this stuff."[7]**
>
> —Amy Gonzales,
> Indiana University Media
> School professor

13

absolutely good or bad. We need to think about how to come up with appropriate uses of this stuff."[7]

How Did We Get Here?

Today's social media landscape has been made possible by advances in computer technology. Laptop computers, tablets, and smartphones all trace their lineage back to the early electronic computers of the 1930s and 1940s. These devices were so big they took up entire rooms. They were slower and had less memory than the computers found in today's wristwatches. But for their time, they were revolutionary. They performed calculations many times faster than human mathematicians could.

Computer technology steadily advanced in the next several decades. Computers became smaller, faster, and cheaper. In 1975, the first personal computers became available. The following year, Steve Jobs and Steve Wozniak released the first Apple computer. Meanwhile, the first word processing program was introduced. By 1983, an estimated ten million personal computers were in use in the United States.

Birth of the Internet

The invention of the internet was the next step toward social media. The internet was first envisioned as a way for US military forces to communicate with each other if the enemy destroyed US telephone lines. Computer networks were connected online by the end of 1969. However, as more and more networks linked up, it became much more difficult for them to work together in a single internet. Fortunately, a breakthrough was just around the corner.

At the end of the 1970s, a computer scientist named Vinton Cerf developed a protocol, or set of rules, that enabled all computers on all smaller networks to talk to one another through the larger internet. Cerf worked for several years to perfect this protocol. On January 1, 1983, Cerf and his coworkers launched the internet. Only government and academic communities used it at first. Cerf convinced the government to allow him to demonstrate how commercial traffic could use the internet. As a result of Cerf's demonstration, three commercial internet providers came into being in 1988 and 1989.

Meanwhile, in 1979 the first dial-up online service for consumers became available. CompuServe provided online access for an hourly fee. This access was between CompuServe users only. Eventually the service offered digital newspaper editions, weather reports, stock market

This 1963 desktop computer weighs more than 100 pounds (45 kg). The manufacturer advertised it as portable, fast, and convenient.

reports, airline ticket booking, and discussion forums. The forums were by far the most popular service. CompuServe customers could communicate with other users via online chat rooms. People with similar interests gathered virtually in topic-based chat rooms to exchange information. Along with the forums, CompuServe initiated e-mail service among its users.

A Motorola engineer made the first mobile phone call in 1973. The first true smartphone, called Simon, went on sale in 1992. In addition to cellular phone service, it could also send and receive e-mails, faxes, and pages; schedule appointments; and keep an address book. It would be another fifteen years before Steve Jobs announced the development of the first iPhone in January 2007.

Social Media Arrives

The 1990s saw social media explode as the first real social media sites came online. Sites such as Six Degrees, Friendster, MySpace, Facebook, and others attracted thousands of users. Most have faded in popularity, but Facebook continues to be an important player in social media.

Facebook went online in 2004, and by August 2015 the social media giant said it had more than one billion daily users. Author and school counselor Ana Homayoun points out that this number accounts for "approximately one out of every seven people on Earth."[8] By June 2017, Facebook had more than two billion active monthly users. At first, Facebook was most popular with college students. Today it would be hard to find anyone of any age, occupation, or educational level in the developed world who doesn't know what Facebook is.

Today's teens may have first used social media on Facebook, but many of them have moved on to use dozens of other apps. Facebook has become less attractive to teens than it used to be, at least partly because it's so popular with older people. When a teen's grandmother or next-door neighbor is posting daily on Facebook, a teen may not be interested in socializing much in that venue. Teens who do still use Facebook tend to use it because it has so many features and because many other apps require users to sign up via Facebook.

EARLY SOCIAL NETWORKING SITES

GeoCities, created in 1994, was one of the first social networking services. GeoCities users could create and customize their own websites. GeoCities grouped these websites into different "cities" based on content. TheGlobe.com launched in 1995. It enabled users to interact with people who had the same hobbies and interests. Users could also publish their own content. Another early social networking site was Classmates.com. When it came online in 1995, its sole purpose was to connect former schoolmates. Eventually the service expanded to include archived yearbooks to accompany its huge directory. Classmates.com is still active today, providing help for organizers of high school reunions.

In 1997, AOL Instant Messenger debuted. Users created profiles that included biographies. The profiles were searchable. That was an innovative feature in the mid-1990s. The social media site Six Degrees launched the same year. It allowed users to upload profiles and make friends with other users. Its name represented the popular theory of six degrees of separation, which claims that any two people can be connected to each other by six jumps from person to person. Six Degrees was not as successful as some other early social networking sites. The site encouraged members to invite more and more people to join. Critics said all the member invitations were spam. SixDegrees.com closed down in 2001.

More than one hundred English-language social media sites are available to teens and adults. Statista, a company that compiles different kinds of statistics, listed the most popular social media services for young people as of fall 2017. At that time, the top five were Snapchat, Instagram, Facebook, Twitter, and Tumblr.

Teens' favorite social media app at the end of 2017 was Snapchat. At least 47 percent of teens surveyed said Snapchat was their favorite. Instagram was second, with 24 percent of teens saying it was their

This smartphone is equipped with several of today's most popular social media apps. They include Snapchat, Instagram, and Facebook.

preferred social media network. Facebook was a distant third, with 9 percent of teens preferring it.

What's the Problem, Anyhow?

More time online appears to lead to an increased risk of problems for teens. Psychologist Lara Jakobsons says, "The more time adolescents are engaged with social media outlets, the higher the risk there is for poor sleep, low self-esteem, and increases in depression or anxiety."[9] The risk may be even greater when teenagers use mostly one service. This increases the pressure and anxiety that teens may experience when they try to be available and up-to-date at all times.

Many parents, teachers, and experts are convinced that teens' use of social media is problematic. Many teens do not agree. Teens may point out that young people have always tried to find ways to get together, talk, plan, and have fun. Teens often say that they don't spend that much time online.

> **"The more time adolescents are engaged with social media outlets, the higher the risk there is for poor sleep, low self-esteem, and increases in depression or anxiety."**[9]
>
> —Lara Jakobsons, psychologist

There are many reasons why teens seem to be so vulnerable to problems with social media use. Even though adolescence has been recognized as a period of human development for centuries, only in the last century has teenagerhood been a defined period of years. According to neurologist Frances Jensen, "The word 'teenager,' as a way of describing this distinct stage between the ages of thirteen and nineteen, first appeared in print, and only in passing, in a magazine article in April 1941."[10]

Teens are often said to be too old for some activities and too young for many others. They are stuck between childhood and adulthood. But it hasn't always been this way for teenagers. Before the twentieth century, adults thought of children as small adults. In many cases, they worked full-time on the family farm. Boys were often apprenticed to artisans. Sometimes children went to live with relatives to work in their households.

The Industrial Revolution of the late 1700s caused a great demand for factory workers, and many children worked long hours in factories, in dangerous conditions, through the 1800s. In the early 1900s, concerned adults began to establish child welfare agencies, which promoted child welfare and labor laws. Some states passed laws controlling child labor, but much of the time, the laws were not enforced. It was only when the Great Depression happened in the 1930s that serious efforts to reduce child labor came about. Compulsory schooling laws also helped teenagers become a group apart from children and adults.

It took the combination of child labor laws and compulsory education laws to create the concept of teenagers. This happened gradually in the mid-twentieth century, from the 1940s to the 1960s. The in-between teen years became less structured. Teens had a lot more time on their hands. They used this time in many of the same ways that teens use their time today. They gathered in groups to talk and be together, whether it was at the local drive-in restaurant or the park or the movie theater.

Teens developed a new culture. They looked different from adults. They dressed differently and had different interests and vocabulary. Author Thomas Hine wrote, "Young people became teenagers because we had nothing better for them to do."[11]

There was disagreement in society about what teens should be doing, which led to many disputes. Adults wanted the teens to act like adults, but the teens no longer had the responsibilities or freedom of adults. Teens wanted adult freedoms, but not necessarily adult responsibilities. This conflict in desires and expectations led to curfews and other ways in which communities tried to control this newly defined group of young people.

Teens have much to learn in the adolescent years. They may struggle to establish separate identities from their families in order to become more independent. This struggle often means that friends

Four teens walk to school together. For many teens, the only ways to gather are at school or online.

become more important than ever before in their lives. boyd writes, "Developing meaningful friendships is a key component of the coming of age process."[12]

Today's teens often have much less physical freedom than previous generations of teens had. Parents worry about robbery, abduction, assault, and dozens of other possible crimes that can happen to their children. It's hard for teens to get together with friends when they are forbidden to walk the mile to a friend's house. Yet teens still want and need to communicate with their friends. They have found a way to do this via their phones, tablets, and computers.

Today's internet-connected teens want to learn how to be adults. They look to their parents as models, and they also look to other adults—including celebrities. They imagine what it would be like to have the freedom that adults enjoy. Teens experiment with freedom by pushing back against adults' expectations. In a teen's eyes, social media is a safe place to try out new ways to express themselves. Sometimes they try out different identities or seek support in the process of coming out as LGBTQ.

Is It All about Friendship?

Parents and other authority figures often blame technology itself for the time teens spend online. However, boyd has a different idea. "Most teens are not compelled by gadgetry as such—they are compelled by friendship. The gadgets are interesting to them primarily as a means to a social end." boyd goes on to say, "Social interactions may be a distraction from school, but they are often not a distraction from learning."[13] Learning takes place in many ways, including what teens learn from each other about social interaction.

> **"Most teens are not compelled by gadgetry as such—they are compelled by friendship. The gadgets are interesting to them primarily as a means to a social end."[13]**
>
> —danah boyd, researcher and professor at New York University and Harvard University

While some teens may indeed have an unhealthy relationship with technology, boyd says that "most of those who are 'addicted' to their phones or computers are actually focused on staying connected to friends in a culture where getting together in person is highly constrained."[14]

Teens could build and maintain their friendships by actually talking on their phones, but most do not. They see their social media activity as more private than phone conversations—or at least more private from their parents, siblings, and teachers. They don't really want privacy from their friends. They want their friends and potential friends to see and hear them. They don't feel the need for adults to hear them. The typical teen attitude toward adults is a kind of paradox, or self-contradictory situation. That is, teens use their parents and many other adults as models, yet publicly teens want to escape adult supervision and influence. This is part of the struggle teens undergo to become independent humans. They want and need adults, but at the same time, teens push adults away.

Parents and teens have different opinions about the need for privacy online. Privacy issues lead teens into many of the most serious problems with social media. They walk a fine line when dealing with privacy online. They want to make and keep friends by being open in their social media activity. Even though many teens know that predators who seek out minors are a danger to them, teens often don't connect that danger with their own freedom to say or post anything online to their friends.

According to Pew Research Center data from 2015, as many as 92 percent of teens go online at least once every day. A whopping 24 percent of teens stay online constantly. They have their phones in their pockets or purses or under their pillows twenty-four hours a day. Teens make mistakes. They have many opportunities to make those mistakes when they are online so much.

Chapter 2

WHAT CAUSES PROBLEMS WITH SOCIAL MEDIA?

Sarah wanted to be online less. She had read that excessive internet use can become an addiction. She didn't want that. Her brother was already in rehab for drug addiction. But every time she tried to leave her phone at home when she went running or just leave it downstairs at night, she felt so rattled. At first she just felt anxious, but as the minutes without her phone wore on, she could think of little else but needing to check Instagram and Snapchat. If she was running, she had to cut the run short to get home to check her phone. If she was in bed, she had to run downstairs to get her phone.

Sixteen-year-old Corrine announced at the dinner table that she needed to have her hearing checked. She wouldn't say why, but her twin brother, Zander, knew it must have something to do with her phone. She had told him last week that she kept thinking that she heard her phone ring, but when she answered, there was no call. Zander told her he bet it had something to do with how many hours she spent on her phone. But she said that was silly—and besides, she wasn't on her phone any more than her friends were.

Is the problem with social media that teens use it too much, or are there other problems too? Most parents say their kids spend too much time online. If that is true, why do teens use social media excessively? Many devote hours a day to their social media accounts. If asked, about half of teens would disagree that they are online too much. They want to stay in touch with friends. And while they might not recognize it, they want to pull away from their family and become more independent. These wants are normal for teens.

Is It the Technology?

Sean Parker was the founding president of Facebook. While Parker is no longer with the company, he has strong opinions about the dangers of the application he helped create. At a November 8, 2017, event, Parker called himself "something of a conscientious objector" to social media. He said, "The thought process that went into building these applications, Facebook being the first of them . . . was all about: 'How do we consume as much of your time and conscious attention as possible?'" Parker added, "And that means that we need to sort of give you a little dopamine hit every once in a while, because someone liked or commented on a photo or post or whatever."[15] Parker also said that he and Facebook cofounder Mark Zuckerberg both understood that they were exploiting a human need for feedback and approval but did it anyway.

> **"The thought process that went into building these applications, Facebook being the first of them . . . was all about: 'How do we consume as much of your time and conscious attention as possible?'"[15]**
>
> —Sean Parker, founding president of Facebook

A study published in 2012 by Diana Tamir and Jason Mitchell supports Parker's statement that a like or comment on a photo or post fills a basic human need. Tamir and Mitchell wanted to find out if disclosing information about oneself is psychologically rewarding. Their study's results showed that humans willingly disclose information about themselves because it triggers feelings of reward and pleasure in the brain. The authors concluded that the human willingness to talk about internal thoughts to others underlines how social humans are. The behavior of talking about ourselves to others is important to our

FACEBOOK RESPONDS TO CRITICISM

Facebook research scientists David Ginsberg and Moira Burke insist, "We want Facebook to be a place for meaningful interactions with your friends and family—enhancing your relationships offline, not detracting from them." To fulfill this goal, Facebook has launched changes to its service. On December 15, 2017, Facebook introduced Snooze. Snooze gives users the option to hide a person, page, or group for thirty days, without having to permanently unfollow or unfriend them.

Facebook has also built a tool it calls Take a Break. Millions of users break up with their romantic interests on Facebook. Research suggests that any kind of contact with an ex is difficult. Take a Break allows people more control over when they see their exes on Facebook, what their exes can see about them, and who can see past posts.

In addition, Facebook has started providing online suicide prevention support. It has introduced artificial intelligence to detect suicidal posts before other users report them. When users report suicidal posts, employees offer the posters a variety of support options. For example, they prompt people to reach out to a friend, offer text that could be used to start a conversation, suggest contacting a help line, and offer live chat with crisis support organizations through Messenger.

Facebook recently pledged one million dollars toward research about the relationships between media technologies and youth development and well-being. It wants to understand how to better support teens as they grow up.

"Hard Questions: Is Spending Time on Social Media Bad for Us?" *Facebook*. December 15, 2017. www.facebook.com.

survival as a species. It helps us create social bonds and alliances. It also helps us get feedback from others so we can know more about them, about what they know, and about ourselves. If a teen gets a good feeling from sharing information through social media, he or she may be more likely to continue using the service and share more.

Likes and Dopamine

The dopamine that Parker mentioned is a brain chemical that the human body produces naturally. This substance is a neurotransmitter, or a chemical messenger in the brain. It sends signals within the brain and to the rest of the body through the central nervous system.

Facebook CEO Mark Zuckerberg participates in a May 2011 conference on web technologies in Deauville, France. Zuckerberg has come under criticism for some aspects of Facebook.

Dopamine has many functions within the body. One of its functions is to regulate how a person experiences pleasure. When a person anticipates something that is desirable, dopamine is released. This causes a person to seek out that desirable activity again and again. Being handed a chocolate ice-cream cone will probably trigger a dopamine release if you like chocolate ice cream. Scientists used to believe that dopamine was released when you began eating the ice cream. Now many researchers believe it is the anticipation of a desirable activity that causes the release. Whatever the timing of the release, dopamine enhances the pleasure of the activity.

Parker says that the likes or positive comments a person receives after posting a message or photo cause a dopamine release. But it may be the anticipation of a like or positive comment that keeps a teen logging on constantly. Parker explained why he helped build Facebook in such a way as to keep those hits of dopamine coming. "It's exactly the kind of thing that a hacker like myself would come up with, because you're exploiting vulnerability in human psychology."[16]

Psychiatry professor Simon McCarthy-Jones wrote about the vulnerability that Parker cited. McCarthy-Jones said, "Humans have a fundamental need to belong and a fundamental desire for social status. As a result, our brains treat information about ourselves like a reward.... Such information is hence given great weight. That's why, if someone says your name, even across a noisy room, it automatically pops into your consciousness."[17]

> **"Humans have a fundamental need to belong and a fundamental desire for social status. As a result, our brains treat information about ourselves like a reward."[17]**
>
> —Simon McCarthy-Jones, psychiatry professor

FOMO

Researchers have reported several other possible reasons why teens may overuse social media. Fear of missing out, informally known as FOMO, is one of the reasons. FOMO describes the worry that others might be having fun while you are left out of that fun. The cure for

THE GOOD AND BAD SIDES
OF BRAIN PLASTICITY

Teens get addicted to substances and behaviors much more quickly than adults do. Neurologist Frances Jensen says that teens, once addicted, "have much greater difficulty ridding themselves of the habit—and not just in their teen years but throughout the rest of their lives." Jensen continues, "It's as if addiction hardwires itself into the brain when adolescents are exposed to substances of abuse."

Human brains are primed to learn from birth onward. The processes of learning and addiction in a teen's brain are similar. A child's ability to learn is partly due to the brain's plasticity. This is the brain's ability to grow and change at any age. Recently scientists found that adults also have brain plasticity, which allows their brains to learn until the day they die.

However, young people's brains have even more plasticity. This capacity for change allows children to learn quickly what they need to know to survive in the world. That aspect of brain plasticity is positive. The flipside: it's easy for teens to become addicted. Smoking is a good example of how easily teens can get addicted. Smoking has declined among adolescents in the past fifteen to twenty years, but 90 percent of new smokers started before they were eighteen. They need less access to an addictive substance or behavior than adults do in order to become addicted.

Frances E. Jensen with Amy Ellis Nutt, *The Teenage Brain: A Neuroscientist's Survival Guide to Raising Adolescents and Young Adults*. New York: Harper, 2015. p. 117.

FOMO is to log into social media to catch up on the latest gossip or news.

A 2015 study by the Pew Research Center reported that 93 percent of US teens fifteen to seventeen years old have access to the internet via smartphone, tablet, or other devices. A 2017 study by Edison Research and Triton Digital reported that North American sixteen- to twenty-four-year-olds spend the most time online via mobile devices. These young people spend an average of nearly two hundred minutes per day online on a mobile device.

With this kind of access to social media, perhaps it's not surprising that teens are afraid of being left out of the loop of social happenings. Ana Homayoun says of teens, "Even those who feel a sense of connectedness may also experience low-grade anxiety about what they might be missing out on if they are not online and available."[18] Other researchers say this low-grade anxiety about missing out can progress to "an absolute terror of exclusion."[19]

Research psychologists Mark Griffiths and Daria Kuss report that higher levels of FOMO are associated with greater time spent on social media services such as Facebook. These higher levels of FOMO may cause lower general mood, lower well-being, and lower life satisfaction. Griffiths and Kuss say that higher FOMO levels may also predict future problems with social media addiction.

Phone Problems

Since the dawn of the smartphone era in 2007, scientists have done a lot of research on whether a person can become addicted to the mobile phone itself. This seems possible, since around 80 percent of time spent on social media is done on smartphones. Research suggests that there are several possible pathways to problematic use

HOM

or and the Silk Road taked

Tor is an internet browser that hides a user's location and activity by bouncing the user's communications around a worldwide network of relays. Tor is one way of accessing the dark web. Silk Road was a black market known for illegal drug sales.

of a mobile phone. Dependence on or overuse of the phone is just one pathway.

Some teens may use their phone in dangerous or prohibited ways. Using their phones to access social media on the dark web can be dangerous. The dark web is a part of the internet that is not searched by common search engines like Google. It is accessible, but it's hidden from users unless they know how to access it. Drug dealing, human trafficking, and other illegal activities are common on the dark web. Anonymous dark web users can track other users. Teens may be caught up in these illegal activities on the dark web.

Some teens get into trouble financially with their phones. Going over data limits due to excessive social media use is one example. Social media can also tempt people to spend more money than they should. For example, teens might impulsively purchase items that they find really appealing or that they think will help them keep up with trends among their friends who are on social media. They might order things and pay for services without understanding the final financial results of their purchases.

Sleep Deprivation

Sleep deprivation is an almost universal result of a teen spending time online. Most teens need at least eight and a half to nine and a half hours of sleep per night to function smoothly. They are still growing, and much of that is done at night. As teens grow, from around age thirteen to eighteen, they slowly change their sleeping habits. They like to go to bed later and get up later. Given the opportunity to sleep in, they will sleep between nine and ten hours a night.

However, most teens have to conform to a different schedule than their bodies prefer in order to attend school or go to jobs. This alone can make a teen lose valuable sleep. Add in the possibility of staying up well into the wee hours to text and post on social media, and sleep deprivation can seriously impair teens' ability to do just about anything. A 2017 study surveyed more than nine hundred adolescents aged twelve to fifteen years old about their sleep habits. One in five of the young people reported that they were "almost always" waking up in the night to check social media or messages.[20]

The National Sleep Foundation says that lack of sleep is one of the most common health risks for adolescents. It can contribute to acne, cause a teen to eat too much, or lead a teen to be aggressive or display inappropriate behavior. A sleep-deprived teen may get sick more easily and is more at risk for drowsy driving. Drowsy driving causes more than one hundred thousand crashes each year.

Too Frazzled to Focus

Teens have always considered themselves able to do more than one thing at once. They may think they can watch TV and do their homework at the same time. They may think they can listen to music while doing anything else. They may do their homework while texting friends, monitoring Facebook, and listening to music.

Schools often give students tablets or laptops that contain all their textbooks, workbooks, and so on. These digital materials force teenagers to be online in order to complete assignments. It's a pretty easy jump from working algebra problems to looking at Facebook when you're already online. In their admirable efforts to be paperless, schools have given teens, especially young ones, more complications than their brains can handle easily. Teens can end up disorganized and discouraged.

Scientists say that while brains are capable of switching rapidly from one subject to another, this is not a productive way to work when both tasks need close focus. Multitasking is particularly difficult for teens because the parts of their brains that control this switching, the parietal lobes, mature late in adolescence.

Nomophobia and Ringxiety

Scientists have been studying another aspect of internet use that they call nomophobia. The term *nomophobia* is short for "no mobile phone phobia." It is the fear of being without one's mobile phone.

Some researchers, such as Nicola Luigi Bragazzi and Giovanni Del Puente, think nomophobia should be a recognized psychological disorder, just as any other phobia might be. Bragazzi and Del Puente explain: "The introduction of mobile phones and new technologies has shaped our daily life, with both positive and negative aspects. . . . Further research is needed . . . to investigate more in depth the psychological aspects of nomophobia and to provide a standardized and operational definition of it.[21] The criteria for diagnosis of nomophobia might include regular and time-consuming use of the phone, which leads to anxiety when the phone can't be accessed. Nomophobia was not recognized in the DSM-V (*Diagnostic and Statistical Manual of Mental Disorders, Fifth Edition*), released in 2013. Bragazzi and Del Puente believe adding it to future editions could advance research efforts in this field of study.

> **"The introduction of mobile phones and new technologies has shaped our daily life, with both positive and negative aspects."[21]**
>
> —Nicola Luigi Bragazzi and Giovanni Del Puente, health researchers

People have coined some new words and phrases to describe aspects of nomophobia. A study done by Daniel Kruger and Jaikob Djerf investigated this phenomenon. The researchers wrote, "Mobile cell phone users have reported experiencing ringing and/or vibrations associated with incoming calls and messages, only to find that no call or message had actually registered." These experiences are sometimes called "ringxiety," "phantom vibrations," "phantom ringing," and "phantom notification."[22]

The Kruger and Djerf study sought to answer a couple of questions. First, could these phantom rings or vibrations be real physical sensations at least some of the time? The researchers contacted several cell phone manufacturers, software providers,

A teen on her smartphone ignores her upset mother. Many teens think their parents are out of touch when it comes to social media.

and network carriers to ask them if their devices and services could explain the phantom experiences. All the companies denied that any issues with their hardware, software, or infrastructure could cause the phantom experiences.

The researchers also wondered: Were certain people more likely than others to experience ringxiety and hear phantom rings? Data revealed that users who worry about abandonment by friends or family are more likely to have these phantom experiences. They also worry that their feelings for a friend or partner are not reciprocated.

Kruger and Djerf found that users who preferred to keep their distance from people emotionally were less likely to experience phantom ringing or vibrating. However, 82 percent of the study's 165 participants had experienced phantom vibrations. Fully 50 percent had experienced phantom notification (on-screen images), and 45 percent had experienced phantom ringing.

Nomophobic users demand constant availability of their phones. They often prefer to communicate via phone rather than face-to-face. Researchers Kuss and Griffiths expanded the definition of nomophobia to include this preference for online contact.

"Nomophobia is inherently related to a fear of not being able to engage in social connections, and a preference for online social interaction (which is the key usage motivation for [social networking sites])." They went on to say that preference for online interaction "has been linked to problematic internet use and negative consequences of technology use."[23]

> **"Nomophobia is inherently related to a fear of not being able to engage in social connections, and a preference for online social interaction."[23]**
>
> —Mark Griffiths and Daria Kuss, research psychologists

Sexting

Sexting is another social media problem that has created a furor. Sexting is the sending of explicit photos or messages via private messaging. Sexting often happens within a potential or existing romantic relationship. Teens and adults may consider it a form of flirting.

The biggest problem with sexting is that it often becomes public, no matter what the senders intended. Snapchat is a popular venue for sexting, mostly because it seems more temporary than other platforms. Photos and videos sent through the service appear for a short time, then disappear. However, nothing posted online can be considered temporary. There are ways for the recipients of these photos and videos to save copies before the messages disappear. Furthermore, sexting has legal, social, and psychological consequences. Snapchat's privacy policy, law enforcement guide, and transparency report state that the company has turned over and will turn over photos and messages to the police if presented with a subpoena, court order, or search warrant.

In 2016, journalist Nancy Jo Sales published the book *American Girls: Social Media and the Secret Lives of Teenagers*. The book explored the ways in which teens are using social media in their daily lives. That year, Sales was interviewed at a public event about her work. The event featured a question-and-answer session, where a thirteen-year-old girl attending the interview shared her thoughts on sexting. The teen felt that her parents were out of touch. They didn't understand that she felt powerful when she sent nude pictures of herself via social media. She felt in control of her body. She thought that parents who worried about their kids sending nude selfies were just like parents of decades ago who were afraid of their kids listening to rock-and-roll. They just didn't understand. This young teen's words reflect what many other young people might say.

Defining the Problem and Its Causes

Maybe smartphones, laptops, and tablets don't cause the problems related to social media. Maybe they are just the devices that allow access to social media. Griffiths and Kuss point out, "It could be argued that mobile phone addicts are no more addicted to their phones than alcoholics are addicted to bottles."[24]

One of the challenges that scientists, counselors, and parents face is determining exactly what does qualify as problematic internet use. Teens have grown up in a world where using technology to communicate is entirely commonplace. They can't imagine life without the connection that social media gives them. This is sometimes called the "always on" lifestyle.[25]

Determining problematic internet use is further complicated by the fact that teens may be online for many hours a day and not exhibit any of the behaviors associated with social media problems. Researchers admit that there is a fine line between frequent and habitual internet use that does not indicate any problem, and the problematic and possibly addictive use of social media. If excessive use of social media does not cause any significant problem in a person's life, then it is hard to call it an addiction.

If social media users develop symptoms and experience consequences that are usually related to substance addictions, it is at least possible that these users are addicted to social media. These symptoms might include changing moods, internal and interpersonal conflicts, tolerance (the need for increasing time on social media), and relapse following an attempt to stop the behavior. These symptoms will be significant enough to disrupt the user's day-to-day life.

While FOMO, nomophobia, and mobile phone overuse may not by themselves cause social media problems, including addiction, researchers believe they may be associated with the possibility of addiction. If teens worry about not being able to connect to their social networks, they may develop impulsive checking habits that may, over time, turn into an addiction.

Technology and Modern Life

Because daily life is so tightly tied in with technology, it can be hard to escape social media and the temptation to use it. Just as social media is tempting, it's also tempting to look at all the hazards of social media and suggest that teens just throw away their phones to avoid these hazards. But that's not realistic. What would happen if parents and schools tried to get rid of all mobile devices? Would this put a stop to the problematic social media use that can become an addiction? Even if such a sweeping solution were possible, it wouldn't work. Teens are tech savvy. They have many ways to stay online even if adults confiscate their phones.

Teens may use the family laptop to get online for homework assignments. It only takes a few minutes to check into their favorite social media sites. They can use tablets the same way. Some teens keep their old phones. Even if the phone service doesn't work, teens can still use the texting and social apps by connecting to wi-fi. Most gaming systems also have chat and messaging features.

Internet use is a fundamental part of modern life. Nomophobia and FOMO among teens are indications of possible internet overuse or addiction. They grow from the basic need of a teenager to interact socially. It may be a need run amok, but it is a need nonetheless.

Do mobile devices cause FOMO, nomophobia, and other issues? Scientists are reluctant to assign a direct effect without a lot more research. Mobile devices are here to stay. Social media is also here to stay. It may not matter whether the devices themselves cause the problems. Solutions will come by learning how to use the devices without falling into the traps they present.

Chapter 3

WHAT HAPPENS WHEN SOCIAL MEDIA USE GOES WRONG?

Fifteen-year-old Tressa confessed that she felt ecstatic when she sneaked a look at her phone during Spanish class and found that she had thirty likes for the photo she posted on Instagram. She said that only one other recent photo had gained that many likes—or at least that many likes during the school day. Sometimes she got fifty likes in the evening or right after school. Her all-time high was seventy-five likes, which she got when she posted a picture of her older brother working out. But when nobody liked her photos, she felt down and depressed. She felt so bad that sometimes she pretended to be sick so she could stay home from school.

Not all psychologists and researchers agree that social media use causes problems for teens. Psychology professor and researcher Sarah Rose Cavanagh disputes another psychologist's claim that smartphones have destroyed a generation. Cavanagh says that psychologist Jean Twenge cherry-picked data to support her conclusion that teens are damaged by social media. Twenge reported her conclusion in a widely read 2017 article in *The Atlantic* titled "Have Smartphones Destroyed a Generation?" Cavanagh points out that even Twenge notes that teenagers today have lower rates of alcohol use, teen pregnancy, smoking, and car accidents than past generations had. "This is what a destroyed generation looks like?" Cavanagh asks.[26]

While social media may not harm all teens, experts generally agree that social media can cause damage to teens depending on how it is used. Just how much is too much is unclear. All teens are different, and they respond differently to social media. Two teenagers may each spend five hours a day on social media. One teen shows no negative effects from these many hours online. The second teen may become anxious, depressed, or even suicidal. It is clear that for at least some teens, there is a tipping point where social media use becomes a problem instead of a pleasure.

How teens spend their time on social media may influence the effects they feel. Psychologists Erin and David Walsh say, "Not all social networking is created equal. It seems that when social networks and the internet are used largely to communicate with family and friends, the resulting social support actually benefits young people's mental health."[27]

However, the Walshes go on to say, "Conversely, extensive use of social networking with 'weak ties' outside of close circles can increase feelings of loneliness and anxiety." When a teen sits for hours scanning the profiles of happy acquaintances, it "could be the depressing equivalent of sitting alone at a party where everyone else seems to be having the time of their lives."[28]

> "Not all social networking is created equal. It seems that when social networks and the internet are used largely to communicate with family and friends, the resulting social support actually benefits young people's mental health."[27]
>
> —Erin and David Walsh, psychologists

Anxiety and depression are the problems most often cited as a result of social media overuse. They both show up in teens' lives in many different ways. Anxiety can be as slight as unease or as severe as panic. Depression may be a temporary down feeling or a long-term hopelessness that can lead to suicide. Anxiety tends to be taken less seriously than depression. "Anxiety is easy to dismiss or overlook, partially because everyone has it to some degree," said Philip Kendall, director of the Child and Adolescent Anxiety Disorders Clinic at Temple University in Philadelphia.[29]

Understanding that these feelings may come from living too much in the virtual world is an important first step for any teen struggling with issues related to social media. Knowing that many other teens face the same problems is important. Discovering that help is available can be lifesaving.

Anxiety

Anxiety is the most common mental health disorder in the United States, according to the National Institute of Mental Health (NIMH). It affects nearly one-third of adolescents and adults. Anxiety has a purpose in that it helps us avoid potentially dangerous situations. However, some people, including many teens, have an overactive fight-or-flight response. They perceive threats where none may exist. When anxiety is overwhelming or constant—when it interferes with daily activities and relationships—it may have morphed from normal anxiety into an anxiety disorder. (Note: Only a professional can formally diagnose anxiety, depression, or another mental health disorder.)

Neuroscientist Frances Jensen writes that teens are worriers by nature. Their brains are still not fully developed and are unable to handle stress consistently. Teens worry about many of the same things. They worry about being socially accepted and about how they are doing in school. They worry about friends, family, health,

Friends jog together in New York City. Exercise can help teens manage stress.

and disasters. Jensen says, "The difference between those with ordinary teenage angst and those with bona fide anxiety disorders is one not of content but of degree."[30]

Stress can be reduced in many ways. Some teens manage stress through coping skills and a supportive family. Others use physical exercise and sports as outlets. If teens do not have physical outlets, coping skills, or some kind of support system, their normal teenage worrying may transform into frightening anxiety or depression or both.

One of the more sinister effects of using social media is the temptation to make comparisons. Even a teen who doesn't overuse social media is likely to feel the sting of comparison. Adults also fall into the trap of comparison—so it's likely that teens, who have less real-world experience, are even more vulnerable to this temptation.

Few teens are going to post a less-than-rosy description of their lives on Facebook or Twitter. They are also unlikely to post an unflattering photo on Snapchat or Instagram. Teens who feel good about themselves may not be bothered by others' false representations. But teens who already have some of the self-esteem issues that are common in adolescence may compare their lives to these carefully curated social media lives and feel sadly lacking. Compared to the lives of teens they see and read about online, their lives seem dull and unattractive. Anxiety and depression may follow.

It makes sense that the more time a teen spends on social media, the more chance there is that he or she will feel overwhelmed by worry and sadness. Psychologist Lara Jakobsons says, "The more emotionally invested [teens] are in one site in particular, the more pressure and anxiety they may experience to be available and up-to-date at all times." Jakobsons goes on to say, "It is common for teens, especially girls, to experience pressure to appear 'perfect' online. The need to appear to have perfect hair, to look skinny or fit, to have the perfect group of friends or the need to get the right amount of likes can consume teens. Not meeting these invisible standards can cause self-loathing and self-doubt."[31]

> **"It is common for teens, especially girls, to experience pressure to appear 'perfect' online. . . . Not meeting these invisible standards can cause self-loathing and self-doubt."[31]**
>
> —Lara Jakobsons, psychologist

A teen's body image can be manipulated in two different ways. One way is by advertising in the media. Many companies are commercially interested in convincing teens that they need the latest products or services to improve their looks. The other way is by teens themselves on social media. Individuals may post images of themselves that are filtered, cropped, and airbrushed. Teens want to present themselves in the best possible light. They often use these carefully altered images to wordlessly promote themselves. Selfies may be a way of saying "Look how thin I am!" or "Look how cool I am!" or "Look how much fun I am!" Such posts can lead teens into competition with each other. They measure themselves by how many positive comments or likes they can get. Likes and positive comments tell them the degree to which they fit in with other teens. This kind of peer pressure can lead teens to believe their looks are inadequate, which can warp their body image and sometimes lead to eating disorders.

Depression

Anxiety may be the most prevalent problem for teens on social media, but depression is the most talked about. The reality is that most of the time the two miseries go together.

Depression is more than just sadness, and sadness is not necessarily depression. There are many reasons that a teen, or any person, might feel sad. Family and school problems, relationship troubles, and a host of other life experiences may cause anyone to feel sad. Teens may be more susceptible to feeling sad than adults are, because teens have less experience in dealing with life's difficulties. The hormonal and emotional turmoil that often accompanies the teen years may worsen teens' sadness.

If a person's sadness or loss of interest or pleasure in most activities persists beyond a couple of weeks, it may be clinical depression or major depression. Depression is much more than feeling a little down. Depressed teens may feel hopeless, gain or lose a significant amount of weight, and have trouble concentrating.

Social media use can be stressful when it leads teens to compare themselves unfavorably with others. This may contribute to depression or anxiety.

They may sleep too much or too little and get headaches and stomachaches. These symptoms are serious enough to interfere with daily life. At its worst, depression may cause recurring thoughts about death and suicidal thoughts, actions, or plans.

Just as with the link between social media use and anxiety, researchers have different ideas about the link between social media use and depression. Clinical psychologists in Great Britain reviewed eight hundred published articles about the connection between social media and depression. They selected thirty studies for closer review. The data used for the thirty studies included more than 35,000 participants between the ages of fifteen and eighty-eight, from fourteen countries.

The results of this review were mixed. Eleven of the thirty studies examined simple correlations between online social networking and depression. Of the eleven studies, 45 percent showed a link between social media use and depression. Meanwhile, 18 percent found that social media has a positive impact on mental health. And 36 percent of the studies found no apparent relationship between social media and depression.

The researchers dug deeper to figure out why the studies produced such different results. The researchers found that social media users suffered the most depression when they felt envy when looking at other social media posts, when they posted frequently (especially with negative status updates), and when they were obsessed about their online identities.

On the other hand, the review also showed that using social media can help people improve their mental health. It can strengthen their social support networks and help people connect to mental health resources.

Bullying

Scientists have invested decades of research into youthful meanness and cruelty. However, researchers have yet to come up with a definition of bullying that satisfies everyone. One of the most widely accepted definitions was proposed by Swedish psychologist Dan Olweus. Olweus named three components of bullying behavior. He said that the behavior must be aggressive and repetitive, and there must be an imbalance of power. He believed that all three of these components must be present for the behavior to be called bullying.

You're ugly

A social media user leaves a mean comment on a teen's photo. Online bullying can have severe effects on victims.

This definition dovetails with the familiar scene of a big kid tormenting a smaller child day after day. Similarly, bullying could also be a popular teenager repeatedly spreading rumors about someone whom peers see as an outcast.

Kids who have been bullied and who also bully others are called bully-victims. Being a bully-victim raises one's risk of mental health, behavior, and social difficulties. Children who are bullied suffer more from anxiety, depression, loneliness, and post-traumatic stress than other children do, and they have a higher risk of suicide. Kids who bully are more likely to experience peer rejection, conduct problems, anxiety, and academic problems than other kids are.

Cyberbullying is a newer version of old-fashioned playground bullying. Cyberbullying is generally defined as using some sort of technology to send mean, threatening, or embarrassing messages to or about another person. This definition of cyberbullying doesn't quite match Olweus's criteria for bullying. Messages may be mean, but meanness alone doesn't make them bullying.

Parents and the news media are inclined to consider any mean or cruel messages—electronic or otherwise—bullying. Teens themselves are much less likely to call these experiences bullying. Teens stick closer to the Olweus criteria for bullying. If mean messages are exchanged between two friends or even just two schoolmates, teens call it drama. This is especially true for girls. The mean messages may be very hurtful, but in most teens' minds the messages aren't a form of bullying.

Researcher danah boyd says of the word *drama*, "Teens regularly used that word to describe various forms of interpersonal conflict that ranged from insignificant joking around to serious jealousy-driven relational aggression."[32] Drama, in a teen's eyes, does not mean that there is a bully and a victim. The persons involved in drama don't have to see themselves as aggressive and powerful or weak and meek. Even when someone is at the center of some sort of conflict, he or she is still able to respond or fight back. Seventeen-year-old Carmen told researchers, "Drama is more there's two sides fighting back. I guess the second you fight back, it's—you're not allowed to call it bullying because you're defending yourself, I guess."[33]

Drama becomes cyberbullying when it meets the Olweus criteria. Someone posts cruel or mean messages to or about a person repeatedly. This person cannot defend himself or herself or reciprocate the cruelty. That inability would happen if the attacked person were less powerful in some way—usually in a social sense.

Cyberbullying may rise to the level of cyberstalking. Cyberstalking is an extreme form of cyberbullying. A cyberstalker is someone who intentionally tries to cause pain or distress in a victim with repetitive, obsessive, long-term harassment. This harassment continues even when the victim has personally warned the cyberstalker to stop. It may be criminal, especially as more laws are enacted to prevent cyberbullying and cyberstalking. This is the kind of aggression that may lead a teen to consider suicide.

Bullying is nothing new. But the power of social media can increase a bully's reach and influence. People can send harassing words and images anonymously. They can spread embarrassing material to all a person's friends with the click of a button. They can bully a victim continuously, night and day, with relatively little effort.

When teens meet on social media, they are fighting for social status. This is a normal—although sometimes painful—experience for teens. They may gossip or engage in drama that can be intentionally or accidentally harmful to others. Not all gossip or drama is a problem, but some of it can be quite hurtful to the teens involved. Social media makes it much easier to engage in this behavior. Teens are often able to distance themselves emotionally from the results of their behaviors.

Predators

Online sexual predation has been widely publicized recently. While sexual predators, usually meaning adult males, certainly exist, some facts about them have been distorted. Parents worry about abduction, molestation, and rape. The stories they read and hear about do not calm their fears. Each new story of abuse motivates policy makers to propose new ways to limit abuse. One of the problems with this approach, according to boyd, is that strangers are unlikely predators. "Most acts of sexual violence against children occur in their own homes by people that those children trust." boyd goes on to say, "Sexual predation did not begin with the internet, nor does it appear as though the internet has created a predatory epidemic. Internet-initiated sexual assaults are rare."[34]

> **"Sexual predation did not begin with the internet, nor does it appear as though the internet has created a predatory epidemic. Internet-initiated sexual assaults are rare."[34]**
>
> —danah boyd, researcher and professor at New York University and Harvard University

Suicide

The Centers for Disease Control and Prevention (CDC) publish statistics about suicide rates. These figures are expressed in terms of the number of suicides per 100,000 people in the population. They show that males aged fifteen to nineteen have historically higher suicide rates than females in the same age group. In 2015, the rate for males of this age was 14.2, and the rate for females was 5.1. This was a sharp increase from 2007 for both groups, when the male rate was 10.8 and the female rate was 2.4.

The years between 2007 and 2015 are also the years when use of social media skyrocketed among teens. Researchers are trying to discover if a direct correlation exists between suicide and increased social media use among teens.

Accidents are by far the most common cause of death for young people aged ten to nineteen. In June 2016, the CDC reported that accidents cause 35.9 percent of deaths in this age group. A large proportion of these deaths result from car accidents. Suicide is the second most common cause of death for this age group at 18.1 percent.

SOCIAL MEDIA AND DISTRACTED DRIVING

According to an American Automobile Association (AAA) study, 6 percent of teenagers aged sixteen to eighteen say it's acceptable to text or e-mail while driving, while 34 percent admit to having done so in the last month. They know it's dangerous, but many do it anyway.

Using social media while driving is just as dangerous. In July 2017, California teen Obdulia Sanchez was driving drunk, speeding, and live-streaming on Instagram simultaneously. She lost control of the car, which crashed and rolled over off the road, killing her fourteen-year-old sister and injuring another teenager. She was charged with vehicular manslaughter, driving under the influence (DUI) of alcohol, and child endangerment, and she was sentenced to six years and four months in prison.

There are three kinds of distracted driving. Visual distraction is taking your eyes off the road. Manual distraction is taking your hands off the wheel. Cognitive distraction is taking your mind off driving. Using social media while driving involves all three of these.

Checking social media, or sending or reading a text or e-mail, takes your eyes off the road for about five seconds. That's long enough to cross a football field while driving at 55 miles (89 kilometers) per hour.

Researchers at the University of Iowa have found what they called an "attentional disengagement" lag that occurs even while someone is simply talking on the phone. Doing two things at once delays responses about four-hundredths of a second. It's a tiny amount of time—but enough to kill when it happens while driving.

Richard Lewis, "UI Study Explores Why Cell Phone Use Leads to Distracted Driving," *IOWANow*, June 5, 2017. now.uiowa.edu.

Distracted driving is one cause of teen car accidents. Checking social media while driving takes a driver's eyes off the road for about five seconds.

Psychologist Jean Twenge is firm in her assertion that a connection must exist between increased social media use and the increase in suicide rates during the last decade or so. Twenge and her associates studied samples of teen surveys taken from 1991 through 2015. They discovered that rates of depression, thinking about suicide, suicide attempts, and successful suicide attempts rose significantly after 2010. This was especially true for females. Twenge points out that the number of teens with mobile phones and the amount of time they spent online increased steadily from 2011 to 2015. Twenge believes there is a correlation.

Twenge says that more research is needed to determine whether the increase in new media screen time is related to the increase of mental health issues after 2011. She says that it is possible that mental health issues increased for some other unknown reason, making these depressed teens more likely to spend time online. However, she does believe that increased screen time is a more likely culprit for the increased mental health problems than some other unknown reason.

Even if there is no direct connection between online time and mental health, Twenge says that online time can still affect mental health indirectly. She says that feeling socially isolated is one of the major risk factors for suicide. If a teen spends more and more time online and less time in face-to-face communication with other people, he or she will eventually feel isolated. If a teen has any other risk factors for depression or suicide, feeling isolated will only raise those risks.

Social media use is only one of many factors that could lead to mental health problems for anyone. Genetic influences, family environments, bullying, and trauma can all play a role. Statistics and risk factors tell only part of the story about suicide, of course. Statistics can never reflect the pain that family and friends feel when a teenager commits suicide. Friends and family members may also feel guilty that they did not do something to prevent their loved one's death. Many of the risk factors for suicide cannot be controlled easily. However, excessive social media use could be. Teens could learn the possible dangers of social media. They could learn how to recognize problems and where to go for help in solving those problems.

SOCIAL MEDIA'S DARK SIDE

Teenagers who are feeling hopeless and wondering why they should keep on living can find much support for their feelings online. Unfortunately, some of that "support" actually encourages teens to commit suicide and shows them how to do it. Social media has a dark side, and suicide is part of it.

Suicide message boards, online chat rooms, forums, and even mainstream social media services provide venues for depressed teens to share their feelings with other teens. Online sharing about suicide is easier than a face-to-face conversation. This is particularly true in a suicide-focused venue, since a teen knows that nobody in a suicide chat room or forum will be shocked by a question he or she might ask.

Some discussion forums idolize people who have committed suicide and even facilitate suicide pacts. Suicide pacts are agreements between two or more people who plan to commit suicide at a particular time, often using the same means. Social media also may encourage copycat suicides. Suicide stories sometimes go viral. The notoriety surrounding a viral story about suicide can be attractive to a depressed and desperate teen.

The support that suicidal teens find online may encourage them to believe that suicide is a valid solution to their problems. Many social media services also offer suicide prevention information, but to despairing teens, the sympathy they find on pro-suicide social media may be more compelling.

Chapter 4

HOW CAN YOU PROTECT YOURSELF AND FIND HELP?

Brittany posted a photo of a boy she likes. She intended for only her best friend to see the photo. However, Callie decided that another friend, Cameron, might help the relationship, so she passed the picture to him. Within minutes Brittany's crush saw the picture. He passed Brittany in the hall without a word. When Brittany realized that Callie had passed the photo along, she was embarrassed and angry. Obviously, Callie was not the good friend Brittany had known for years.

It may seem that to avoid all the dangers and pitfalls of using social media, the surest solution would be to retreat completely from any online use. But this is not a realistic approach to the problem. This is a digital age. Schools often use the internet to communicate with students. Many teachers require online research and let students submit schoolwork online. Parents find digital access helpful in communicating and coordinating schedules with their children. For teens, one of the most important benefits of internet access—and social media use in particular—is being able to make and maintain friendships with other teens online. Some of these friends are ones they see every day at school, while others are friends they may never

Many teens use social media for purposes other than socializing. This has become apparent in many ways. Four young survivors of the February 2018 school shooting at Marjory Stoneman Douglas High School in Parkland, Florida, have used social media to drive attention to their campaign for gun control. Emma Gonzalez, David Hogg, Cameron Kasky, and Jaclyn Corin all survived the shootings that killed seventeen other students and staff members at the school. The four have used Facebook, Instagram, and Twitter to spread their message. They organized a national school walkout day and a subsequent march in Washington, DC, to advocate for more effective gun laws. Hundreds of thousands of people turned out for both events.

Another example of online activism took place in a different way several years earlier. Reddit, a social news, rating, and discussion site, has many subgroups in which users with similar interests can post and chat. A *Minecraft* subgroup community talked a teen out of committing suicide in 2014. After posting his intent to commit suicide, the young man was flooded with messages of support from fellow users in the Reddit *Minecraft* community. More than fifty community members used TeamSpeak software to talk to the young man directly. Several hours later, the young man posted that their support had helped him feel better. He was no longer considering suicide.

see in person. How can teens fulfill their need to belong without experiencing the worst of social media's downsides?

Privacy

Privacy is a word that comes up often in conversations about social media. danah boyd says of privacy, "It is a process by which people seek to have control over a social situation by managing impressions, information flows, and context."[35]

Privacy online seems like a simple enough idea. To maintain privacy, keep personal data private—period. But teens have many different opinions about what needs to be private. Much of the trouble happens when two teens have different ideas.

boyd says cynics often suggest that only people who have something to hide need privacy. This is not true, because people—teenagers in particular—need privacy to develop and grow. Privacy is especially important for teens who feel like they don't fit in. Those marginalized teens can often find the support and acceptance they need online, even when they can't find it in their real-world daily lives. Teens want to participate in some of the public aspects of social media, but they also look for ways keep certain things private within those public spaces.

How can teens walk that line between privacy and their need to express themselves? One of the most straightforward ways to control privacy is to examine privacy settings closely for any social media service and to check them regularly. Social media privacy policies are constantly changing. A teen may not even know when the policies change, or when friends change settings in ways that affect others. Friends whose posts were always set for "friends only" might change their settings to public. Comments you made to those friends are now available for everyone to see, regardless of whether that was your intent. Author Margarita Bertsos says of online privacy, "And even if your own account is private, remember nothing's ever truly private online."[36]

> "Even if your own account is private, remember nothing's ever truly private online."[36]
>
> —Margarita Bertsos, author

It's not unusual for teens to have only a vague understanding of what constitutes privacy in a given app. They may say they want privacy but only mean

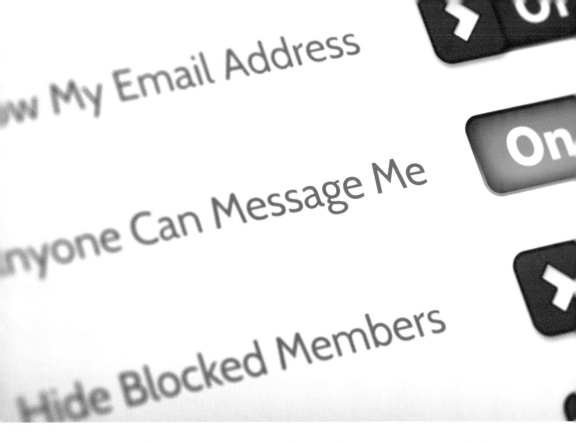

Social media privacy settings can be complicated and may change unexpectedly. It is important to check them often.

privacy from parents or certain other people. They see no problem with companies like Facebook collecting data about their lives, including what products or services they use. Facebook and other social media companies use this data to target advertisements for these products or services. On the surface this seems harmless enough, but collected data can be used in surprising and problematic ways.

Don't assume anything when it comes to privacy settings. The following examples show how privacy settings can be tricky or confusing. Instagram is a very popular social media platform. The photos and videos people post can be made private, but the default setting is public. Tumblr, a scrapbook of text, photos, and video and audio clips, is a bit like Twitter and a bit like a blog. A Tumblr profile can be made private, but only through what one author calls an awkward workaround. The first profile a Tumblr user creates is public. Anyone on the internet can see it. Users who want privacy have to create a second profile, which they can protect with a password. Snapchat is a popular messaging app because users can put time limits on photos or videos they send. When the time's up, the posts disappear. Teens often use Snapchat to send embarrassing or goofy photos because they don't think these photos can be made public. However, Christine Elgersma of Common Sense Media says, "It's a myth that Snapchats go away forever."[37] Snapchats can be recovered. Also, receivers of Snapchat messages can take screenshots of the images. These are only a few of the apps in which privacy settings can be misleading. Check those settings, and check them often.

> **"It's a myth that Snapchats go away forever."[37]**
>
> —Christine Elgersma, Common Sense Media

The dangers of sexting are related to the vague or nonexistent notions of privacy that teens sometimes have. Journalist Judith Johnson says, "When a girl gets a request from a boy for a nude photo, she might think it's because he likes her. Sadly, her nude photo will probably just give some boy bragging rights for putting another notch on his belt. Stimulating each other's raging hormones is not empowering, it is a dangerous game."[38] It is a game that can escalate offline. Teens may decide to meet in person. Sexting involves an impression of distance and safety. That safety is not present offline. In spite of what teens may think, the situation can intensify and cause untold harm.

How can teens avoid some of these serious issues? Janell Burley Hofmann, author of the book *iRules: What Every Tech-Healthy Family Needs to Know about Selfies, Sexting, Gaming, and Growing Up,* suggests using what she calls the T.H.I.N.K. rule. Is your post true? Hurtful? Inspiring? Negative? Kind? She says, "The important thing is to know you're making a choice every time you engage with social media."[39]

"The important thing is to know you're making a choice every time you engage with social media."[39]

—Janell Burley Hofmann, author of *iRules*

The bottom line, according to Hofmann, is to think about who you want to be offline in real life. Make sure that your choices do not sabotage that goal. While you might want to look good online, recognize that nobody's perfect. You don't need to appear perfect online any more than you need to be perfect offline.

To protect yourself from online sexual predators, use the same common-sense measures you use to control any other aspect of social media. Maintain your privacy settings. Stop to think before you friend someone that you don't know in real life. Never agree to meet anyone in person alone, no matter how tempting it may be.

Staying Focused

Learning to be organized, both online and offline, can help you stay focused and be more successful academically. There are many apps to help with organization of both text and time. These include Forest, which keeps you locked out of your phone for a time period you choose, and myHomework, which is an all-in-one school planner. Homayoun says that a teenager should also use at least one written planner. Research evidence shows that writing out anything helps a person remember it.

Homayoun also advocates trying dual screens. Assign one screen for work and one screen for socializing. Also, find ways to avoid

Social media can make it hard to stay focused on schoolwork. Separating homework time from social media time is one way to improve focus.

toggling from one page to another, which may be necessary when you're using the same device to read text and complete a worksheet. Switching screens constantly disrupts focus. Split screens may work for some teens.

Getting Enough Sleep

When you are tired all day after staying up late to post new pictures on Instagram, the answer, however hard, may be to turn the phone off at bedtime. Psychologist Amy Green says that the temptation for teens to bring their cell phones to their bedrooms is a strong one. Research suggests that some teens form strong attachments to their phones. They feel separation anxiety when parted from their phones either physically or by turning off the phones.

A compromise may be needed to separate teens from their phones at night. Parents can make sure teens know the problems with sleep deprivation and make sure that nothing else is causing their teens to wake up in the night. At that point, parents and teens can negotiate to determine a reasonable bedtime that requires turning off the phone or leaving it in another room overnight.

Where to Get Help

If a teen has crossed the line into serious problems with online use, where can that teen turn for realistic advice? Many teens turn to their peers for help. Peer support has great value for teens; it helps them develop social skills and cope with stress. However, these friends may have similar problems, they may not be aware of all the relevant issues and resources, and their still-developing brains may not be able to offer advice based on sound judgment. Fortunately, most teens know that they need to reach out to trusted adults in addition to peers.

Lately many celebrities have spoken out about helping teens cope with distress caused by social media. Melinda Gates is a businesswoman and philanthropist. Gates said in a 2017 *Washington Post* article, "I spent my career at Microsoft trying to imagine what technology could do, and still I wasn't prepared for smartphones and social media."[40] Gates went on to encourage parents and teens to learn about the issues. She recommended watching a documentary called *Screenagers.* She says that parents have told her they like the film because it provides plenty of practical tips.

First Lady Melania Trump promised to make the fight against cyberbullying one of her priorities. In a September 21, 2017, appearance at a luncheon for spouses of United Nations world leaders and committee heads, Trump urged adults to take the lead in teaching the world's children "life's many ethical lessons." The First Lady condemned bullying both "online and in person." She spoke of

When social media use leads to serious problems, teens can turn to parents, teachers, and other trusted adults for help. They can also find useful information from advocacy organizations online.

the need to address "the message and content [children] are exposed to on a daily basis through social media."[41]

Teens can find online resources to help them with bullying. For example, Stopbullying.gov provides information from various government agencies on what bullying is, what cyberbullying is, who is at risk, and how schools and students can prevent and respond to bullying. Stopbullying.gov details what bullying looks like in a series of warning signs. Most bullied young people will exhibit some of these signs. They include frequent headaches, stomachaches, and changes in eating habits. A bullied student may also have trouble sleeping and not want to go to school. The website also offers tips for standing up to bullies, such as using humor to deflect the bully. Tips include knowing when to walk away and when to say "stop" with confidence.

Stomp Out Bullying is a national antibullying and anticyberbullying organization for US kids and teens. The organization's motto is Stomp Out Bullying: Change the Culture. It educates people on the need for civility, inclusion, and equality for all young people. It teaches solutions on how to respond to all kinds of bullying. The Stomp Out Bullying help chat line is the centerpiece of the organization's online resources. It is a free and confidential help chat for teens. It supports all young people who have been victims of any kind of bullying. Trained counselors are available during scheduled hours to lend support to any teens who feel distressed because they are being bullied.

The Jed Foundation is a nonprofit organization that exists to protect emotional health and prevent suicide for our nation's teens and young adults. The organization partners with high schools and colleges to strengthen their mental health, substance abuse, and suicide prevention programs and systems. It offers many resources designed to help teens and young adults with the skills and support to become healthy, thriving adults. The Jed Foundation was formed in 2000 by Donna and Phil Satow, who lost their son Jed to suicide. They hope to provide models for schools about how to prevent suicides. The website provides expert resources, several different signature programs for schools, and recent news relating to student suicide and substance abuse.

The nonprofit organization Common Sense Media is a valuable resource for all kinds of information about several different forms of social media. It offers ratings as to age appropriateness and content, reviews from adults and kids, and all the latest news about technology changes and how they affect families.

Helpguide.org is a website that offers online guidance on mental and emotional health, including the "Teenager's Guide to Depression: Tips and Tools for Helping Yourself or a Friend" (www.helpguide.org/articles/depression/teenagers-guide-to-depression.htm). This guide offers help for recognizing depression and its causes, as well as tips for overcoming teen depression. It contains a long list of other resources for young people who need more options.

Crisis Text Line is a free, around-the-clock crisis support service available by text to anyone in the United States who needs help with a painful emotion. A user texts the word "HOME" to 741741 to connect with a trained volunteer crisis counselor. The counselor uses active listening and collaborative problem-solving to help the user to a calmer, safer state of mind. For more information, visit www.crisistextline.org.

That's Not Cool is an education initiative that partners with young people to address dating violence, unhealthy relationships, and digital abuse. Digital abuse includes unwanted repeated calls or text messages; privacy violations such as breaking into email or social networking accounts; and pressure to send nude or private pictures or videos. An interactive website (www.thatsnotcool.com), innovative apps and games, and many other tools help teens learn to recognize, avoid, and prevent dating violence in their lives; practice healthy relationship skills; and draw their own digital boundaries.

It appears that social media use can cause some of the problems that teens face. But how much is too much when it comes to social media use is perhaps unknowable, because it depends so much on the teen's individual nature and circumstances. The future world of today's teens is highly unlikely to be any less virtual than their present world is. When teens become anxious, depressed, or even suicidal; when their grades decline; when their physical health is affected, adults must find ways to help teens navigate their increasingly digitized world. Their futures depend on it.

MOST POPULAR SOCIAL NETWORKS WORLDWIDE

Network	Users (millions)
FACEBOOK	2,234
YOUTUBE	1,500
WHATSAPP	1,500
FACEBOOK MESSENGER	1,300
WECHAT	980
INSTAGRAM	813
TUMBLR	794
QQ	783
QZONE	563
SINA WEIBO	392
REDDIT	330
TWITTER	330
BAIDU TIEBA	300
SKYPE	300
LINKEDIN	260
VIBER	260
SNAPCHAT	255
LINE	203
PINTEREST	200
TELEGRAM	200

AS OF APRIL 2018

RANKED BY NUMBER OF ACTIVE USERS (IN MILLIONS)

"Most Popular Social Networks Worldwide as of April 2018, Ranked by Number of Active Users," *Statista*, 2018. www.statista.com.

RECOGNIZING SIGNS OF TROUBLE

How can you know if social media use is causing problems for you? One problem might be that you are spending too much time online. Another problem could be that what you are reading online is causing you anxiety or depression. The following are a few clues that might help you see if social media use is a problem for you.

What are signs you are spending too much time on social media?

- The amount of time you spend on social media is enough that it has a negative impact on your studies or your job.
- You spend a lot of time thinking about social media or planning how you will use it.
- You try to cut down on your social media use, but you can't seem to do it.
- You feel the urge to use social media more and more.

What problems or situations may be caused by social media?

- You feel unable to go to school because you don't want to leave your home.
- You sometimes feel hopeless about your life.
- You become restless or troubled if you are not able to access social media.
- You realize that you are using social media in order to forget about your personal problems.

ORGANIZATIONS TO CONTACT

Jed Foundation

www.jedfoundation.org

The Jed Foundation is a nonprofit organization that works to help teens and young adults with mental health issues.

Mental Health America

www.mentalhealthamerica.net

Mental Health America is an organization that seeks to promote mental health as an important part of overall wellness.

National Suicide Prevention Lifeline

www.suicidepreventionlifeline.org

The National Suicide Prevention Lifeline provides free, confidential counseling online and over the phone to people undergoing suicidal crises.

Pew Research Center: Internet and Technology

www.pewinternet.org

The Pew Research Center's analysis of the internet and technology provides up-to-date information about how people use smart devices and social media.

Stopbullying.gov

www.stopbullying.gov

The US government's Stop Bullying site provides resources for preventing and stopping cyberbullying.

SOURCE NOTES

Introduction: The New Virtual World

1. Judith Johnson, "Teens Addicted to Social Media," *The Huffington Post,* December 6, 2017. www.huffingtonpost.com.

2. Jean Twenge, "Have Smartphones Destroyed a Generation?" *The Atlantic,* September 2017. www.theatlantic.com.

Chapter 1: What Are the Problems with Social Media?

3. Sarah Williams, "Are Behavioral Addictions the Same as Drug Addictions?" *MentalHelp.net*, November 26, 2015. www.mentalhelp.net.

4. danah boyd, *It's Complicated.* New Haven and London: Yale University Press, 2014, p. 78.

5. danah boyd, *It's Complicated*, p. 79.

6. Kyle Smith, "Why Teens' Addiction to Screens Isn't as Bad as Parents Fear," *New York Post,* September 3, 2017. nypost.com.

7. Natalie Jacewicz, "Social Media Bad for the Minds of Young People, Right? Maybe Not," *USA Today*, October 7, 2017. www.usatoday.com.

8. Ana Homayoun, *Social Media Wellness.* Thousand Oaks, CA: Corwin, 2018, p. 27.

9. Lara J. Jakobsons, "Social Health: Teenagers' Mental Health and Social Media," *Northshore University Healthcare System*, September 25, 2017. www.northshore.org.

10. Frances Jensen, *The Teenage Brain: A Neuroscientist's Survival Guide to Raising Adolescents and Young Adults.* New York: Harper, 2015, p. 16.

11. Thomas Hine, "The Rise and Decline of the Teenager," *American Heritage*, September 1999. www.americanheritage.com.

12. danah boyd, *It's Complicated*, p. 17.

13. danah boyd, *It's Complicated*, p. 18.

14. danah boyd, *It's Complicated*, p. 18.

Chapter 2: What Causes Problems with Social Media?

15. Jessica Chasmar, "Ex-Facebook President Bashes Social Media: 'God Only Knows What It's Doing to Our Children's Brains,'" *The Washington Times*, November 9, 2017. www.washingtontimes.com.

16. Simon McCarthy-Jones, "Are Social Networking Sites Controlling Your Mind?" *Scientific American,* December 8, 2017. www.scientificamerican.com.

17. Simon McCarthy-Jones, "Are Social Networking Sites Controlling Your Mind?"

18. Ana Homayoun, *Social Media Wellness*, p. 16.

19. Daria J. Kuss and Mark D. Griffiths, "Social Networking Sites and Addiction: Ten Lessons Learned," *International Journal of Environmental Research and Public Health,* March 17, 2017. www.ncbi.nlm.nih.gov.

20. Amy Green, "Should Bedrooms Be No-Phone Zones for Teens?" *Psychology Today,* February 17, 2017. www.psychologytoday.com.

21. Nicola Luigi Bragazzi and Giovanni Del Puente, *A Proposal for Including Nomophobia in the New DSM-V*, May 16, 2014. www.ncbi.nlm.nih.gov.

22. Daniel J. Kruger and Jaikob M. Djerf, "High Ringxiety: Attachment Anxiety Predicts Experiences of Phantom Cell Phone Ringing," *Cyberpsychology, Behavior, and Social Networking,* January 2016. deepblue.lib.umich.edu.

23. Daria J. Kuss and Mark D. Griffiths, "Social Networking Sites and Addiction: Ten Lessons Learned."

24. Mark D. Griffiths and Daria J. Kuss, "Adolescent Social Media Addiction (Revisited)," *Education and Health Journal*, 2017. sheu.org.uk.

25. Daria J. Kuss and Mark D. Griffiths, "Social Networking Sites and Addiction: Ten Lessons Learned."

Chapter 3: What Happens When Social Media Use Goes Wrong?

26. Sarah Rose Cavanagh, "No, Smartphones Are Not Destroying a Generation," *Psychology Today,* August 6, 2017. www.psychologytoday.com.

27. Erin Walsh, M.A. and David Walsh, Ph.D. "It's Complicated: Teens Social Media, and Mental Health," *Psychology Today,* September 28, 2017. www.psychologytoday.com.

28. Erin Walsh and David Walsh, "It's Complicated: Teens, Social Media, and Mental Health."

29. Benoit Denizet-Lewis, "Why Are More American Teenagers Than Ever Suffering from Severe Anxiety?" *The New York Times Magazine,* October 11, 2017. www.nytimes.com.

30. Frances E. Jensen with Amy Ellis Nutt, *The Teenage Brain.* New York: Harper, 2017, p. 201.

31. Lara J. Jakobsons, "Social Health: Teenagers' Mental Health and Social Media."

32. danah boyd, *It's Complicated*, p. 137.

33. danah boyd, *It's Complicated*, p. 138.

34. danah boyd, *It's Complicated*, pp. 110–111.

Chapter 4: How Can You Protect Yourself and Find Help?

35. danah boyd, *It's Complicated*, p. 76.

36. Margarita Bertsos, "Will Your Posts Come Back to Haunt You?" *Scholastic Choices,* November–December 2017. choices.scholastic.com.

37. Christine Elgersma, "17 Apps and Websites Kids Are Heading to after Facebook," *Common Sense Media*, July 15, 2017. www.commonsensemedia.org.

38. Judith Johnson, "Teens Addicted to Social Media."

39. Margarita Bertsos, "Will Your Posts Come Back to Haunt You?"

40. Melinda Gates, "Melinda Gates: I Spent My Career in Technology. I Wasn't Prepared for Its Effect on My Kids," *The Washington Post,* August 24, 2017. www.washingtonpost.com.

41. Suyin Haynes, "Melania Trump Urges Adults to Teach Children About Cyberbullying 'By Our Own Example,'" *Time,* September 21, 2017. www.time.com.

FOR FURTHER RESEARCH

BOOKS

Sean Covey, *The 6 Most Important Decisions You'll Ever Make: A Guide for Teens*. New York: Touchstone, 2017.

Claire Edwards, *Social Media and Mental Health: Handbook for Teens*. Newark, Nottinghamshire, UK: Trigger Press, 2018.

Thomas McDonagh and Jon Patrick Hatcher, *101 Ways to Conquer Teen Anxiety: Simple Tips, Techniques, and Strategies for Overcoming Anxiety, Worry, and Panic Attacks*. Berkeley, CA: Ulysses Press, 2016.

Andrea C. Nakaya, *Internet and Social Media Addiction*. San Diego, CA: ReferencePoint Press, 2015.

Andrea C. Nakaya, *Is Social Media Good for Society?* San Diego, CA: ReferencePoint Press, 2017.

Justin W. Patchin and Sameer Hinduja, *Words Wound: Delete Cyberbullying and Make Kindness Go Viral*. Minneapolis: Free Spirit Publishing, 2014.

Jacqueline B. Toner and Claire A. B. Freeland, *Depression: A Teen's Guide to Survive and Thrive*. Washington, DC: Magination Press, 2016.

INTERNET SOURCES

Elizabeth Chuck, "Is Social Media Contributing to Rising Teen Suicide Rate?" *NBC News*, October 22, 2017. www.nbcnews.com.

Benoit Denizet-Lewis, "Why Are More American Teenagers Than Ever Suffering from Severe Anxiety?" *New York Times Magazine*, October 11, 2017. www.nytimes.com.

Hayley Krischer, "It's 10 P.M. Do You Know What Apps Your Children Are Using?" *New York Times*, September 6, 2017. www.nytimes.com.

WEBSITES

Common Sense Media

www.commonsensemedia.org

This website provides independent reviews, age ratings, and other information about several types of media: movies, books, TV, games, apps, and websites.

Helpguide.org

www.helpguide.org

This site, created in partnership with Harvard Health Publications, offers more than 160 informative and engaging articles covering twenty-one mental, emotional, and social health topics, from abuse to suicide prevention. It also provides self-help tools.

Project Semicolon

www.projectsemicolon.com

This organization is devoted to helping reduce the incidence of suicide through connected communities and greater access to information and resources.

INDEX

IMAGE CREDITS

ABOUT THE AUTHOR

Bonnie Hinman has written more than fifty books, most of them nonfiction for middle school readers. Hinman was sobered by the statistics on suicide among teens. She is a social media user and now pays more attention to how much time she spends on Facebook. She lives in southwestern Missouri, near her children and their families. She has five grandchildren who will become teens over the next few years. Hinman's discoveries about the problems with social media will be passed on to them.